# CIRRHOSIS COOKBOOK MANUAL

## Diet For Cirrhosis Of The Liver; What To Eat And Avoid

## EVVA WORKMAN

# Table of Contents

# CHAPTER ONE

# DIET FOR CIRRHOSIS OF THE LIVER

## Cirrhosis Diet: What to Eat and Avoid

If you have cirrhosis, your daily diet and hydration habits are critical.

To help those with cirrhosis who may become malnourished due to changes in their metabolism and digestion, a cirrhosis diet has been developed.

As a result, what you eat and drink every day is critical if you have this condition. When you have cirrhosis, your liver may not be able to keep up with the demands placed on it by foods high in protein, sodium, and sugar.

As part of your healthcare team, registered dietitians can help you design a diet for people with liver disease. This will ensure that you are well-nourished and avoid making decisions that could lead to weight gain or other health issues.

Benefits

One of the most important organs is the liver, which performs more than 500 functions.

1 To perform one of its most important functions in a damaged liver, the liver is unable to efficiently obtain nutrition from the food that you eat, due to cirrhosis.

When you have cirrhosis, your liver has to work harder than it should, which increases the risk of complications and further liver damage. Cirrhosis-related complications, such as death, are more common in people with liver disease who are malnourished, according to research.

There is no one-size-fits-all approach to managing cirrhosis' diet, according to a 2018 article published in the Journal of Clinical Gastroenterology. Early initiation of a cirrhosis diet is critical for a better prognosis and treatment outcome.

As it stands, cirrhosis scarring can't be reversed. You can take control of your health and your future with diet if you suffer from liver cirrhosis.

## Its Mechanisms

It's important to customize your cirrhosis diet based on your personal health and nutritional requirements, but the following general dietary guidelines can serve as a starting point:

A person with cirrhosis should abstain from alcohol in any form, as it increases the risk of further liver damage and, in the worst case scenario, liver failure. Malnutrition and other health issues can also result from excessive alcohol consumption.

The liver produces bile, a yellow-green fluid, which the body uses to digest fats. Digestive symptoms may occur when the liver is damaged, as the production and supply of bile may be affected. A high-fat meal is harder to digest for a liver that isn't functioning properly. (In moderation, healthy fats can be included.)

Raw or undercooked meat and seafood should be avoided because cirrhosis patients have weakened immune systems, making them more susceptible to foodborne illness.

Additionally, you may need to alter the quantity of food that you consume. You may need to eat more calories per day to meet your body's increased energy demands if you have liver disease, which increases your risk of malnutrition. 5

When it comes to protein intake and liver disease, there is no one size fits all solution. Protein's role in hepatitis is still being debated and researched. 6

Your doctor or a nutritionist will be able to tell you exactly how much protein you should eat. Protein is critical in preventing muscle atrophy because of its high caloric content and diverse nutritional value (thinning). 7

If you have liver cirrhosis, your doctor may advise you to make additional dietary adjustments to help manage or prevent other conditions.

## Duration

Even if you don't feel ill, your doctor may advise you to follow a cirrhosis diet if you have a family history of liver disease. A person in the compensated phase of liver disease has no symptoms at all.

# CHAPTER TWO

If you've been diagnosed with liver disease, you may not notice any symptoms for a long time because the damage to your liver is so severe (decompensated phase).

8 Cirrhosis diets can only help prevent further liver damage, but they can't reverse the damage that's already been done, so you'll likely need to stick with them for some time.

Eating Routines

When it comes to a cirrhosis diet, there are certain foods and drinks you must abstain from at all costs. But you can choose from a wide variety of nutrient-dense and delectable foods, such as fresh fruits and vegetables, whole grain products, and plant-based protein sources.

## Compliant

• Vegetables and fruits; (raw or cooked without butter, oil, or salt)

eggs and egg whites

- Fish that has been prepared in the traditional manner (salmon, tuna)

- Skinless, boneless poultry (without the skin)

- Greek low-fat yogurt

cheeses such as ricotta and cream cheese

- Cheeses with a strong flavor, such as cheddar (cheddar, mozzarella)

Fruit and nut butters (unsalted)

Beans and other legumes, dried

• Butters made with nuts (unsalted)

• Tofu

dairy products that have been fortified (almond, soy, rice)

• Margarine

• Oats

Cereals and crackers made with whole grains

- Rice made from brown rice

- Extra virgin olive oil

Herbs that have been freshly harvested

- Non-dairy milks

- Garlic

- Ginger

- Quinoa and couscous.

- Bars made of granola or cereal

- Water from coconuts

- Approved meal/supplement supplements

Non-Compliant

- Fish and shellfish that have been partially or completely raw (e.g., oysters, clams)

Frozen foodstuffs, fast food

- Red meat

- Preserved foods in cans (meat, soup, vegetables)

• Packaged and processed food (incl. frozen)

sausage, hot dogs and lunch meat are all examples of foods that can be served.

Preservatives, such as sauerkraut and pickles

• Buttermilk

Tobacco product, such as paste or sauce

• Oatmeal, instant hot cereal, etc.

popcorn, rice cakes, pretzels, potato chips

The refined white flour pastas, loaves, and rices

trans fat and partially hydrogenated oils (palm oil, coconut oil)

• Mixes for breading, coating, and stuffing

• Dairy products with all of their natural fat

• Baking mixes for loaves, biscuits, pancakes, and other sweets

• Cakes, cookies, muffins, doughnuts, and other baked goods

Parmesan, Swiss, blue and feta cheeses are all included in this category.

# CHAPTER THREE

frosting and custard mixes

a variety of seasonings, such as sea salt or table salt

Salad dressing and steak sauce are examples of condiments

soups and sauces made with bouillon cubes

Tea, coffee, and soft drinks that contain caffeine

• Alcohol

Choose fresh fruits and vegetables whenever possible, as canned foods are often high in sodium and sugar. The addition of fruit to your breakfast cereal or oats will provide additional nutrition, fiber, and a touch of natural sweetness. Apples, which are high in fiber, can be eaten as a healthy snack on their own.

Full-fat dairy products are likely to be too difficult for your body to process, so avoid them. Greek yogurt, low-sodium hard cheese, and fortified milk alternatives like almond or soy are your best bets for a healthy diet.

Pudding, custard, and ice cream, all of which contain milk as an ingredient, should be restricted. It's possible that you may need to completely avoid them if your body has a hard time breaking down fat and sugar.

Make your own bread, pasta and brown rice from whole grains rather than refined white flour. As long as they're low in sugar and sodium, granola and granola bars are acceptable as quick snacks.

A cirrhosis diet does not allow red meat, nor any processed lunch meat or sausage. Salmon, fresh-caught fish (like sardines), and egg whites may be suitable for those with a calorie restriction.

Dried beans and legumes, small amounts of unsalted nuts or nut butter, and tofu should make up the majority of your protein intake.

There are many ready-made desserts that are high in sugar and salt; therefore, it is best to avoid them. Unless you can make your own low-fat, low-sugar, and low-salt pastries, doughnuts, and muffins, you should generally avoid them.

If you have liver cirrhosis, you can't drink alcohol, but there are plenty of other options. When it comes to hydration, water is the best option, but if you're watching your sodium intake, be sure to read the labels on any bottled water you purchase. Pasteurized milk and juice are only safe to eat.

Most doctors recommend that patients with cirrhosis avoid all caffeinated beverages, including coffee, tea, and soft drinks, even if some studies have shown that coffee may have health benefits for people with alcohol-related liver disease.

## Is this the best time?

If you have liver disease and are undernourished, your doctor may advise you to eat more food.

9 Small, frequent meals and snacks throughout the day can

help you eat more calories if you don't feel like eating large meals.

People with liver disease may experience sleep disturbances, including night terrors. Long periods of uninterrupted sleep are possible, but they may also need to take a nap during the day. People with cirrhosis who wake up in the middle of the night may benefit from a late-night snack, according to research. This is especially true if the snack is specially formulated.

Your meals should be planned around when you are awake, regardless of whether it's during the day or night. A meal or snack should not be skipped for more than a couple of hours at a time.

## Cooking Suggestions

If you don't like using oil or butter to cook your vegetables, try grilling or boiling them instead.

If you're on a cirrhosis diet that requires you to reduce your sodium intake, consider substituting fresh herbs and spices for table salt. Salt substitutes may be an option if you find it difficult to give up your habit of sprinkling salt on food.

When preparing meat, choose lean cuts first. Instead of eating red meat, opt for skinless poultry instead.

Depending on the preparation, you may be able to eat small portions of beef on occasion. Cirrhosis diets require a lower fat content, so grilled meat is a better option than frying it in oil or butter.

Additional measures can be taken to reduce the risk of foodborne illness by adhering to proper food handling and safety practices.

## Modifications

If you experience ascites, hypoglycemia, or encephalopathy as a result of your cirrhosis, you may need to change your diet.

10 In the event that you are diagnosed with one or more of these conditions, your healthcare provider may recommend that you make additional dietary changes.

Ascites

Ascites is a condition in which the abdomen is filled with fluid. People with cirrhosis and ascites are often told by their doctors to follow a low-sodium diet, because salt can exacerbate their condition. 11

People with ascites should consume 88 millimoles per liter (mmol) of sodium daily.

11 Every day, the average American consumes between 200 and 300 milligrams of sodium.

Prepackaged and ready-to-eat foods are often high in sodium or contain additional salt. Not checking nutrition labels on a regular basis can leave you unaware of your sodium intake.

# CHAPTER FOUR

Buying fresh produce, lean meats, and low-fat dairy near the store's perimeter—all of which are low in sodium—is a good rule of thumb when it comes to shopping. The middle aisles of the grocery store are full of prepackaged snacks, cereals, and sodas.

Encephalopathy

The body produces ammonia when it breaks down protein. This is easily eliminated when the liver is functioning properly. A damaged liver, on the other hand, is unable to process even the normal amount of protein.

Ammonia levels rise in direct proportion to the amount of protein being digested. Toxic at high concentrations, it can lead to memory loss, dementia-like symptoms and a potentially deadly complication known as encephalopathy.

Cirrhosis patients should substitute meat for plant-based protein sources when planning their daily menus. It's possible that your doctor will set a daily or mealtime protein restriction for you.

## Affecting the Brain: Hepatic Encephalopathy and Liver Disease

## Hypoglycemia

Cirrhosis patients often suffer from hypoglycemia, or low blood sugar, which is another common symptom of the disease. Glycogen is a simple sugar that your liver can store energy from when you eat complex carbohydrates.

Cirrhosis impairs your liver's ability to store chemical energy. This can lead to low blood sugar in people with liver disease.

People with cirrhosis who suffer from hypoglycemia may benefit from eating meals high in fiber and low in glycemic index, according to research.

## Considerations

To avoid further liver damage, it's critical that you follow your cirrhosis diet exactly. There are general principles you can follow to help you succeed in this endeavor.

A cirrhosis diet emphasizes a focus on whole, unprocessed foods. You may be prescribed vitamins or nutritional supplements by your doctor because your condition makes it difficult to maintain a healthy diet. Particularly if you are experiencing nausea or other GI symptoms, this is a good rule of thumb to follow.

# CHAPTER FIVE

Many vitamin A supplements and multivitamins are toxic to the liver because of the amount of vitamin A they contain.

In high doses, iron can be difficult for the liver to metabolize. Talk to your doctor about any supplements or vitamins that may interact with your medication or cause gastrointestinal symptoms.

You should approach the cirrhosis diet as a positive lifestyle choice to promote your health, because dietary changes are critical. This means that when you go grocery shopping, you should pay attention to the fat, sugar, and salt content labels to ensure that you are making the healthiest possible choices. The following are examples of possible scenarios:

Gluten-free bread, pasta and crackers if you have celiac disease.

• A cirrhosis diet should avoid high-protein legume and bean pastas.

Limiting the amount of protein you get from plant sources like nuts, seeds, and tofu.

With careful planning and shopping, fresh produce, dried beans, and other ingredients for healthy cirrhosis diet recipes can be affordably obtained. You'll save money while avoiding foods that worsen cirrhosis thanks to this plan.

If you're on a cirrhosis diet, remember to include meals you get while out to eat. When you're out to eat, don't be afraid to inquire about the menu options.

A cirrhosis diet plan can be tailored to your specific needs with the help of a registered dietitian or nutritionist, as well as your doctor.

A cirrhosis diet plan is only as effective as the support you receive from your family and friends. This is especially true if you have advanced liver disease and may require assistance with meal preparation and planning.

A support group for people with liver disease in your area might be a good place to get information about a cirrhosis diet that works for you. It's also possible to find cirrhosis diet menu ideas online through message boards, social media hashtags, or blogs by patients.

Take into consideration the cost of nutritional supplements and Ensure when your healthcare provider recommends them. A prescription for these supplements may be possible if you have health insurance. Some of the additional nutrition costs may be paid for by the government.

An Item of Speech

Cirrhosis can make it difficult to maintain a healthy diet. Your body's energy requirements may necessitate varying your intake of certain foods.

It's also critical that you keep an eye on your diet to avoid further liver damage. Alcohol, high-fat foods, and raw or partially cooked shellfish are a few of the things you'll want to stay away from.

However, if your liver is already diseased, changing your eating habits can improve your quality of life and help you avoid further complications.

Antioxidant-rich vitamins, such as vitamin C and vitamin E, may aid in liver health. One of the most important ways to keep your body healthy is by making sure you get enough vitamin D. Remember that a damaged liver may be particularly vulnerable to the toxic effects of certain vitamins (or an excess of them).

Polyphenol-rich fruits have been shown to protect the liver.

14 Strawberry, pomegranate and grapes are some of the fruits that provide these advantages. Polyphenols are abundant in a wide variety of plants and herbs.

• How can cirrhosis be cured as quickly as possible?

Cirrhosis is an incurable disease for which there is no treatment.

Medical and lifestyle changes may be necessary, as well as liver transplantation, to treat liver disease. 15 For those who have cirrhosis, a cirrhosis diet can help to slow the progression of the disease.

THE END

www.ingramcontent.com/pod-product-compliance
Lightning Source LLC
Chambersburg PA
CBHW051403150726

48000CB00003B/1314